75347246 9

D1799803

WILDLIFE WORLDS

SOUTH AMERICA

Tim Harris

W

FRANKLIN WATTS

LONDON • SYDNEY

Franklin Watts
First published in Great Britain in 2019 by The Watts Publishing Group
Copyright © The Watts Publishing Group, 2019

HB ISBN: 978 1 4451 6732 9
PB ISBN: 978 1 4451 6731 2

Printed in Dubai

Series Editor: Amy Pimperton
Series Designer: Nic Davies smartdesignstudio.co.uk
Picture researchers: Rachelle Morris (Nature Picture Library),
Laura Sutherland (Nature Picture Library), Diana Morris

Picture credits:
Alamy: Dani Carlo/Prisma/Dukas Presseagentur GmbH 21bl.
Dreamstime: Agami Photo Agency 15b; Anky10 25tl; Maria Luisa Lopez Estivill 19c; David Havel 8br, 31t; Izanbar 25tc;
Laura Kanda 10; Jesse Kraft 14bl; Mikelane45 22bl; Ondrej Prosicky 23bl; Jeremy Richards 21tr; Gabriel Rojo 26bl;
Scanrail 1, 23br; Sietebravo 3t, 11c; Taani65 22br.
FLPA Images: Malcolm Schuyl 19br.
Nature PL: Oriol Alamany 28; Theo Allofs 22–23; Juan Manuel Borrero 27t Mark Bowler 25bt; Lucas Bustamante 19tr;
Bernard Castelein 17c; Murray Cooper/Minden 12; Christophe Courteau 7c; Jack Dykinga 21c; Nick Hawkins front cover
t; Daniel Heuclin 8bl; Chien Lee/Minden 25bl; Luiz Claudio Marigo 16; David Noton 2b, 18–19c, 20; Pete Oxford 8–9c,
17bc; Michael Pitts 29bl; Michel Roggo back cover tcl, 24; Gabriel Rojo 15tr, 26c, 27bl; Andy Rouse 11t; Cyril Ruoso
15tl; Kevin Schafer 7tr;
Roland Seitre 27br; Visuals Unlimited 13bl; David Welling 9tr; Staffan Widstrand 23tr; Bert Willaert 17br.
Shutterstock: abriendomundo 21br,31b; Audrey Snider-Bell 9br; tamara bizjak 11bl; Ger Bosma Photos 13tr, 30b; buteo
back cover tl, 7tl; Patrick K Campbell 6b; Ecuadorpostales 14c; Dirk Ercken front cover b, 4b; Andrey Golinkevich 6–7;
guentermanaus 13tl; Lukasz Kurbiel 2t, 17t, 30c; Lucas Leuzinger back cover tcr, 4c, 30t; Lulilel front cover c; Don
Mammoser 3cr, 11br; MarcusVDT 3br, 25tr; Veronika Maskova 5c; Carlos Mauer 29tr; Vadim Petrakov 5t; Anton Petrus
3bg, 4–5bg, 29t, 30bg; Eduardo Rivero 29br; Miroslaw Skorka 19tl; Super Prin back cover tr, 5b, 13br; Wollertz 17bl.

Franklin Watts
An imprint of
Hachette Children's Group
Part of The Watts Publishing Group
Carmelite House
50 Victoria Embankment
London EC4Y 0DZ
An Hachette UK Company

www.hachette.co.uk
www.franklinwatts.co.uk

With thanks to the Nature Picture Library

Contents

South American Continent

South America is almost completely surrounded by oceans. Its only land link is the Isthmus of Panama, which connects it to Central America. South America's incredible geography boasts the longest mountain range (Andes, 7,200 kilometres) and the biggest river by water volume (Amazon), which is surrounded by the world's largest rainforest.

South America is a continent of extremes. Some places near the Pacific coast of Colombia are among the rainiest locations on Earth, while it never rains in parts of the Atacama Desert. The continent's varied landforms and climates, and the fact that large areas have suffered little human disturbance, mean that South America's nature is very diverse. There are more kinds of bird and amphibian than in any other continent, though many are endangered.

More than 2.5 million species of plants and animals are believed to live in the Amazon Rainforest alone. Scientists think this figure could be even higher.

JAGUAR

GOLDEN DART FROG

CENTRAL
AMERICA

Angel Falls has the highest
uninterrupted drop of any waterfall.

NORTH
ATLANTIC
OCEAN

ANGEL FALLS

Isthmus of Panama

Llanos

ORINOCO RIVER

Tepuis

Guiana Highlands

Cotopaxi

EQUATOR

Galápagos
Islands

AMAZON RIVER

Amazon Rainforest and
Amazon River Basin

BRAZIL

Andes Mountains

Altiplano

The Pantanal is
the world's largest
freshwater wetland.

Lake Titicaca

Atacama
Desert

PARAGUAY RIVER

PARANÁ RIVER

Iguazú
Falls

Valle de
la Luna

IGUAZÚ RIVER

Salar de
Atacama

SOUTH PACIFIC
OCEAN

Laguna
Miscanti

ARGENTINA

PARANÁ RIVER

Pampas

SCARLET MACAW

Pampas

At 6,962 metres,
Aconcagua is
the continent's
highest mountain.

SOUTH
ATLANTIC
OCEAN

Torres del
Paine

Llanos

Stretching from the Colombian foothills of the Andes Mountains to the delta of the Orinoco River in Venezuela there is the Llanos – a vast area of tropical grassland, occasionally broken by patches of forest.

For much of the year it is dry, but when heavy rains start in April the tributaries of the Orinoco burst their banks and the area becomes a series of huge, shallow lakes. These are perfect feeding areas for birds and reptiles, including the world's most powerful snake, the green anaconda.

Up to 300,000 herons, storks, wildfowl and shorebirds feed on the Llanos wetland. As the waters recede in the dry season, the lakes shrink and the birds feed closer together.

Green anacondas are not venomous, instead they squeeze the life out of their prey. They can kill animals as large as deer and capybara.

The capybara is the world's largest rodent. It spends most of its life in water.

When they mature, river dolphins (especially the males) turn pink.

A giant anteater has an incredibly long, sticky tongue, with which it can pull up to 30,000 ants a day from their nests.

Tepuis

In the Guiana Highlands of northern South America is a series of large, flat-topped mountains called tepuis. The word means 'house of the gods' in the language of the local Pemon people.

The tepuis are made of tough, ancient sandstone and tower high above the surrounding rainforest. The plant and animal life on the mountaintops is very different from that in the forest below. Some plants growing at the summits exist nowhere else on Earth. There are no large animals at the top, but plenty of birds, frogs and mice.

On the lower slopes of the mountains, pale-throated sloths sleep for up to 20 hours each day, hanging from branches. When they do move, it is very slowly.

Beautifully marked but highly venomous, the fer-de-lance lives in the forests below the tepuis.

The waters of the Churún River plunge 800 metres from the top of the Auyán-tepui over the Angel Falls. This is the world's highest waterfall.

Goliath birdeaters are the heaviest spiders in the world. They eat frogs, small mammals, and lizards, but only rarely do they kill birds.

Galápagos Islands

Lying either side of the equator in the Pacific Ocean, these islands have been created by millions of years of volcanic eruptions and are composed of volcanic lava. Almost all the reptiles, most of the land birds and one-third of the plants are found nowhere else.

The islands' reptiles include giant Galápagos tortoises, which can live to more than 100 years old. Many seabirds raise their young on the islands, including Galápagos penguins, which are the only members of their family to swim north of the equator.

Galápagos penguins hunt small fish in the cold, nutrient-rich Cromwell Current during the day and return to the islands at night.

Sally Lightfoot crabs are brightly coloured scavengers living on the shore.

A male blue-footed booby dances, showing off his blue feet to impress a female. Bluer feet are more attractive to females.

Marine iguanas graze on algae growing on underwater rocks, then swim ashore to warm themselves in the sunshine.

Amazon Rainforest

The world's largest tropical rainforest – the Amazon – covers an area of 6 million square kilometres, which is ten times the size of France. The Amazon contains 390 billion trees of 16,000 different kinds.

Nowhere else on Earth has such a variety of life. Among its 2.5 million animal and plant species, rainbow-coloured macaws and other parrots squawk as they fly through the forest canopy. Up here, monkeys and sloths stay hidden most of the time, anxious to avoid the hunting harpy eagles. Down below, crocodiles and piranhas search for prey in rivers, while jaguars and ocelots (wild cats) prowl the forest floor.

The Amazon River drains the rainforest, carrying its excess water to the Atlantic Ocean. The river carries more water than the next seven biggest rivers put together.

The transparent wings of glasswing butterflies help to camouflage them from birds and other predators.

Piranhas have sharp teeth and strong jaws to eat the flesh of animals unlucky enough to get too close!

Colourful poison-dart frogs live in bromeliads, which are plants that grow on tall rainforest trees.

Red, yellow and blue – and very noisy – scarlet macaws eat seeds, nuts and fruit growing on forest trees.

Andes Mountains

Stretching 7,200 kilometres from the southern tip of Argentina to the north of Colombia, the Andes form the longest range of mountains in the world.

There are thousands of snow-capped peaks, including active volcanoes, as well as glaciers and deep canyons. The highest parts of the range are treeless, but below the treeline there is cloud forest. This is home to an extraordinary variety of mammals, amphibians, invertebrates and birds, including tanagers, hummingbirds and woodpeckers.

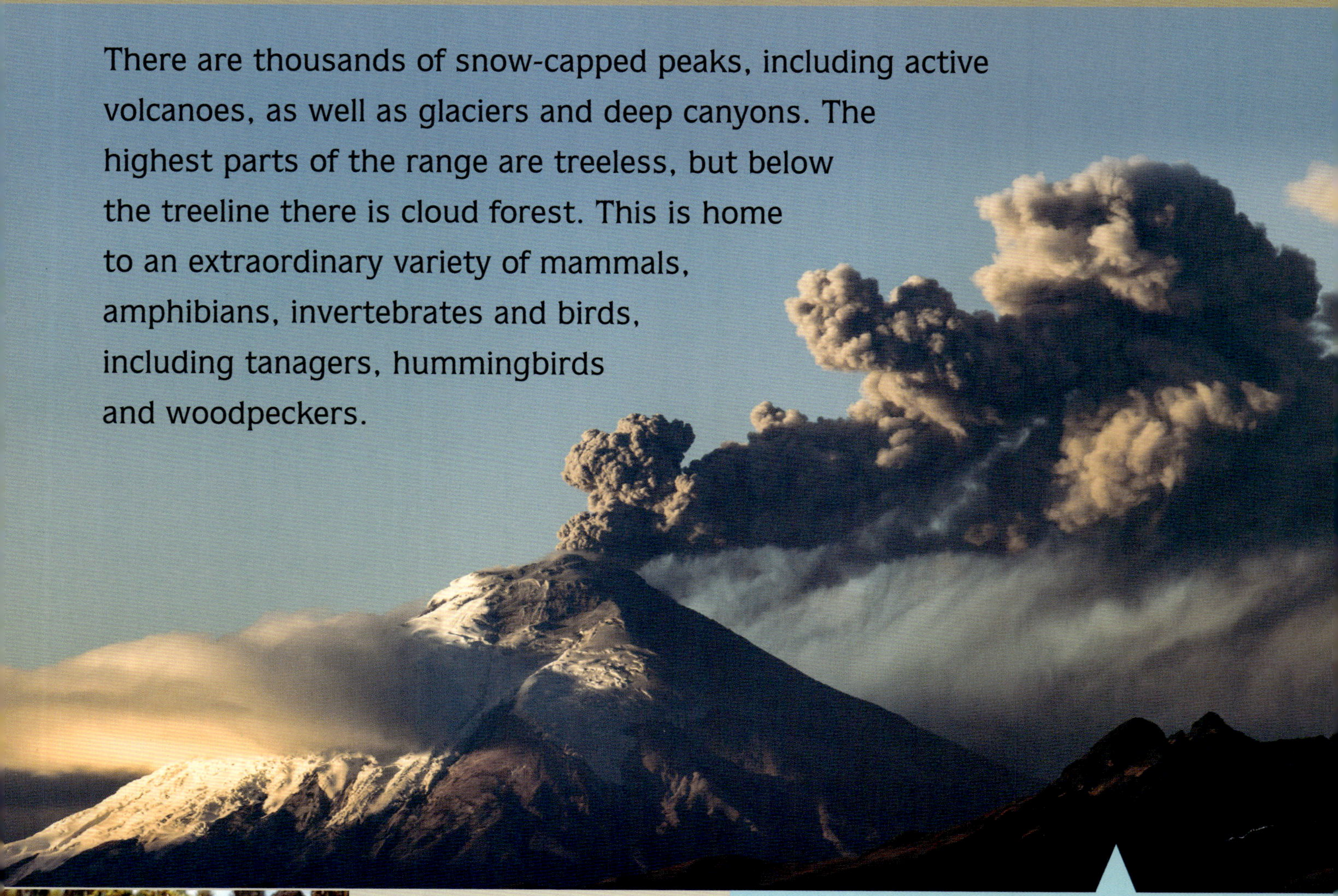

Espeletias grow high in the Andes. These plants have thick trunks that absorb water from clouds that drift by at these high altitudes.

Famous peaks in the Andes include Aconcagua and Cotopaxi (above), which is one of the world's highest active volcanoes. At 6,961 metres, Aconcagua rises higher than any other mountain outside of Asia.

Shy vicuñas live in herds on mountain slopes up to 4,800 metres. People sometimes shear them for their very fine wool.

The Andean cock-of-the-rock is a cloud forest bird. Males display their brilliant plumage in groups called leks; bowing and flapping to attract the attention of females.

Andean condors are the largest flying land birds in the world. They often glide 200 kilometres in a day in search of dead animals (their favourite food), rarely flapping their wings.

Lake Titicaca

Lake Titicaca is an extraordinary body of fresh water. As well as being the largest lake in South America, it is also the highest of the world's largest lakes, at 3,800 metres above sea level.

Situated high in the Andes Mountains, the lake has many rivers draining into it, but only one, the Desaguadero River, flows out. Reedbeds and other aquatic vegetation grow around the margins, providing sheltered places for fish and frogs to breed and for birds to build their nests. Almost all of Titicaca's fish species live nowhere else in the world.

Isla del Sol ('Is and of the Sun') is the largest of the 41 islands in the lake. Most of its residents are farmers and fishers. The island's many ruins date back hundreds of years to the Inca civilisation.

Culpeos, or Andean foxes, hunt small animals, such as rabbits and hares.

The cantuta has pink, trumpet-shaped flowers. It is the national flower of Peru.

Local people build boats and even houses from the totora reeds that grow around the lake.

Titicaca water frogs spend most of their lives at the bottom of the lake. Like all frogs, their skin can absorb oxygen from the water.

Altiplano

The Altiplano ('high plain') is a vast windswept plateau of grassland, sparkling white salt flats and lakes, such as Laguna Colorada, high above sea level. Oxygen levels in the air are only half those at sea level.

The Altiplano lies between two massive ranges of the Andes in Bolivia and Chile. Many of the surrounding mountains are active volcanoes. Although warm by day, temperatures often plunge below freezing at night. It rarely rains. Despite the difficult conditions, many animals live here, including llamas, vicuñas and alpacas. The lakes attract large flocks of flamingos and ducks.

Laguna Miscanti lies in a hollow surrounded by bunch grass below the extinct volcano of Cerro Miscanti. The lake is more than 4,000 metres above sea level – even higher than Lake Titicaca.

One of the rarest birds in the world, the Andean flamingo breeds at just a few shallow lakes, including Laguna Colorada.

Spectacled bears are generally solitary animals. They eat mostly plants, though they also kill and eat rabbits and other small animals.

CERRO MISCANTI

The Andean hillstar hummingbird feeds on the nectar of flowering plants, including cacti.

Like all cacti, the candelabra cactus thrives in arid places. It grows up to 6 metres tall, has a spiny trunk and tubular white flowers.

Atacama Desert

Sandwiched between the Andes Mountains and the Pacific Ocean in northern Chile is the driest desert on Earth. On average, only 1.5 centimetres of rain falls each year. No rain has fallen for many years in some places.

Despite the arid climate, over 500 different kinds of plant have been found growing in the desert. Cacti and succulents can store what little water is available to help them survive. Hardy scorpions, beetles and lizards eke out an existence. Humboldt penguins live along the Pacific shore and flamingos breed at the saline lakes that form in the Salar de Atacama.

The Valle de la Luna (Valley of the Moon) is named for its similarity to the surface of the Moon.

With its long ears and hind legs, a viscacha looks like a rabbit with a long bushy tail.

Burrowing owls roost in holes in the ground. They often move into burrows abandoned by viscachas.

The Fabian's lizard is found only in the Salar de Acatama, a huge salt flat in the Chilean Atacama.

If rain does fall, plants sprout and bloom as if by magic in a vivid show of colour called the *desierto florido* ('desert bloom').

21

Pantanal

Covering an area over 180,000 square kilometres, the Pantanal is the world's largest freshwater wetland. It lies on the floodplain of the Paraguay River, which drains much of southern Brazil.

When heavy rains fall between November and March, vast areas of grassland and forest are flooded. Water levels fall during the dry season, but many swamps and marshes remain. These are home for millions of waterbirds and caimans, as well as big cats, crab-eating foxes and marsh deer.

Pig-like tapirs are excellent swimmers and divers.

With its wings spread, the sunbittern is an unmistakable bird. It flashes the spots on its wings to startle predators.

Water levels rise by about 5 metres in the wet season. Some areas are completely flooded with water, in other areas large lakes appear.

The biggest of the wild cats living in South America, jaguars are capable of killing any other animal living in the Pantanal except for the largest caimans.

Up to 10 million yacare caimans live in the Pantanal. This is the largest population of crocodilians anywhere in the world.

A toucan's distinctive beak is designed to help lose body heat, which helps to keep the bird cool.

Iguazú Falls

On the border of Argentina and Brazil, the mighty Iguazú River flows over a layer of very hard basalt rock. When the water reaches the edge it crashes 82 metres into a chasm called the Devil's Throat.

The Iguazú Falls are one of the biggest waterfall systems in the world. On average, 100 million litres of water – enough to fill 40 Olympic swimming pools – flows over them every minute. The spray soaks the surrounding area, nourishing the forest. In turn, the trees provide homes for frogs, insects, birds and other animals.

When water levels are high in the Iguazú River, it may plunge over as many as 300 separate falls, producing clouds of spray as it roars through the Devil's Throat.

Ring-tailed coatis are members of the raccoon family. They are equally at home on the ground or clambering around in trees.

Many kinds of butterfly live near the falls, including species of callicore or 'eighty-eight'. They are named for the markings on the underside of their wings.

The harpy eagle is a powerful bird. It can seize a monkey from the forest canopy and fly away with it.

Black capuchin monkeys are among the most intelligent of New World monkey species.

The sting of a bullet ant is the most painful of any insect.

Pampas

Stretching from the foothills of the Andes Mountains to the Atlantic coast in Argentina is a vast plain of grassland called the Pampas. The word *pampa* means 'flat surface' in Spanish.

Although many of the original coarse (rough) grasses have been replaced by those more suitable for the domestic cattle that graze here, the Pampas is still important for many wild mammals, birds and reptiles. Large wildfires burn the grass regularly, but it recovers quickly.

26

Pampas foxes live in dens in hollow trees or in abandoned burrows dug by other animals.

Darwin's rhea is flightless, but can run at 60 kilometres per hour if escaping a predator. Male birds incubate the eggs and guard the chicks for around six weeks after hatching.

Cortaderia selloana, also simply called pampas grass, is native to the region. It can reach 3 metres in height and has distinctive white feathery plumes.

About the size of a domestic cat, Geoffroy's cat hunts alone at night.

Torres del Paine

Close to the Pacific coast in the far south of Chile is one of the most spectacular landscapes on Earth. The Torres del Paine are jagged granite peaks that tower over the surrounding countryside.

The Torres del Paine National Park is named for these impressive peaks. The Spanish word *torres* means 'towers'.

The national park also contains glaciers, lakes, glacier-cut valleys and many other snow-covered mountains, whose summits are often hidden in cloud. Cougars are the top predators of the park, whose other residents include guanacos and endangered deer called huemul.

The Cuernos del Paine rise more than 2,000 metres above Lake Nordenskjöld. Cuernos means 'horns' in Spanish.

The black and bright red plumage of the magellanic woodpecker is very distinctive. These large birds eat invertebrates that live in trees.

Guanacos are swift-running, hardy animals that are also strong swimmers.

Commerson's dolphins are small, but very active marine mammals. They often leap from the water and spin in the air. Sometimes they swim upside down.

Glossary

algae very small plant-like life-forms

aquatic living in water

arid very dry

basalt hard and usually dark type of volcanic rock

canopy the uppermost branches of the trees in a forest

chasm a deep, steep-sided crevice in the ground

cloud forest a forest that is covered with low-lying clouds for much of the time

current water that is moving in one direction

delta the area where a river drops its sediment as it enters a lake or the ocean

dry season the part of the year when very little rain falls

endangered species of plant or animal that is at risk of becoming extinct

eruptions explosive blasts from volcanoes

extinct not active (volcano); died out forever (animal or plant)

floodplain the flat area either side of a river that may flood when water levels in the river are high

glacier a large body of ice moving slowly down a valley

Inca a civilisation that lived in western South America from 1438 to 1533

incubate to sit on an egg to keep it warm before it hatches

invertebrate an animal without a backbone

lava hot, molten rock that erupts from a volcano

marine of or from the ocean

nectar sugary liquid found in flowers

New World a group of monkey species that are native to South America, which is known as the New World. (Old World monkeys exist in Africa and Asia.)

plateau high, level ground

plumage a bird's feathers

predator animals that hunt and kill other animals

prey animals that are eaten by other animals

recede to move back

salt flat flat land covered with a layer of salt where water has evaporated

solitary alone

succulents plants with thick fleshy leaves or stems that store water

summit the very top

tropical relating to the tropics, the areas above and below the equator

venomous producing chemicals that can injure or kill prey

Books

Animal Families (series) by Tim Harris (Wayland, 2014)
Close-up Continents: Mapping South America by Paul Rockett (Franklin Watts, 2016)
Infomojis: Continents by Jon Richards and Ed Simkins (Wayland, 2019)
Journey Through: Brazil by Liz Gogerly and Rob Hunt (Franklin Watts, 2017)
Natural Wonders of the World by Molly Oldfield (Wren & Rook, 2019)

Websites

South America Facts for Kids
Lots of interesting and fun facts on Brazil.
www.kids-world-travel-guide.com/brazil-facts.html

Geography for Kids
Has profiles of every country in South America.
www.ducksters.com/geography/southamerica.php

Go Wild
Discover more about your favourite
animals in these WWF fact files.
gowild.wwf.org.uk/americas

National Geographic Animal Pictures and Facts
Simply type in the animals you're interested in and get
lots of fascinating facts. Covers mammals, reptiles,
amphibians, fish and birds.
www.nationalgeographic.com/animals/index/

Note to parents and teachers:
Every effort has been made
by the Publishers to ensure
that the websites in this book
are of the highest educational
value, and that they contain
no inappropriate or offensive
material. However, because
of the nature of the Internet,
it is impossible to guarantee
that the contents of these
sites will not be altered. We
strongly advise that Internet
access is supervised by a
responsible adult.

Further information

Index